☞ **W9-AGG-236**

629.4
GAF

Gaffney, Timothy R.

Kennedy Space
Center.

33197000039474

DATE			
10-23			
12-19			
2-19			
3-19			
7-25			

FLINT LAKE MEDIA CENTER

DISCARDED

BAKER & TAYLOR BOOKS

A New True Book

KENNEDY
SPACE CENTER

By Timothy R. Gaffney

CHILDRENS PRESS ®

CHICAGO

Artist's drawing of what a space station might look like.

PHOTO CREDITS

JFK Space Center—2, 4, 10, 18, 26, 32, 35, 41

NASA—Cover, 8, 9, 13 (left), 23 (left), 29, 33, 34 (2 photos), 36, 37 (left), 39, 40, 41, 42, 43

National Air and Space Museum—12 (2 photos), 13 (right), 23 (right)

U.S. Fish and Wildlife Service—15, 16

Sovfoto—20 (right), 24

Jet Propulsion Laboratory—20 (left)

Finley-Holiday Films—37 (right)

Len Meents—7

COVER—Huge crawler carries space shuttle and its rocket to the launchpad.

AP/Wide World—43, 45

Dedicated to Mark

Library of Congress Cataloging in Publication Data

Gaffney, Timothy R.
  Kennedy Space Center.

  (A New true book)
  Includes index
  Summary: Describes the history and work of the
John F. Kennedy Space Center located on Merritt Island
on the east coast of Florida.
    1. John F. Kennedy Space Center—Juvenile literature.
[1. John F. Kennedy Space Center. 2. Space flight]
I. Title.
TL4027.F52J638   1985   629.47'8'0975927   85-11317
ISBN 0-516-01269-X   AACR2

Copyright ©1985, 1987 by Regensteiner Publishing Enterprises, Inc.
All rights reserved. Published simultaneously in Canada.
Printed in the United States of America.
  3 4 5 6 7 8 9 10 R 94 93 92 91 90 89 88 87

TABLE OF CONTENTS

BLAST-OFF

It is a quiet morning on Merritt Island in Florida. Sunlight gleams on marshes and ponds. Near the seashore, a tall rocket sits on a raised concrete pad.

The rocket breaks the stillness with a mighty roar. Flames leap from its engines. Seconds later, the rocket climbs into the sky, leaving a trail of smoke.

MERRITT ISLAND

Merritt Island is the home of the John F. Kennedy Space Center. It is where America launches astronauts into space.

Kennedy Space Center is located along the east coast of Florida. The water between Merritt Island and the coast is called the Indian River. Beyond Merritt Island is the Atlantic Ocean.

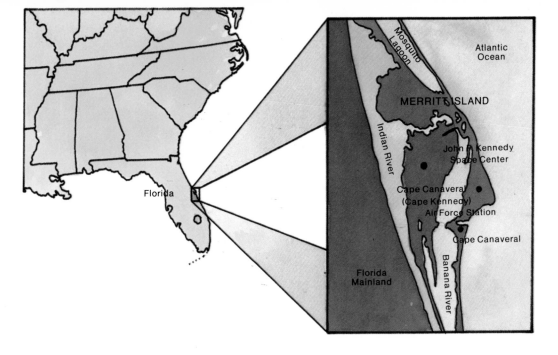

Just to the south of Merritt Island is Cape Canaveral and the Cape Canaveral Air Force Station. The space center was once on Cape Canaveral. The first American astronauts took off from there.

The *Columbia* was America's first space shuttle.

Rockets are still launched from Cape Canaveral. But space shuttles take off from Merritt Island. A space shuttle is a rocket with wings like an airplane. Space shuttles also can land on Merritt Island, on a special runway.

Discovery glides to a landing at the Kennedy Space Center.

SPACE SHUTTLES AND SATELLITES

Kennedy Space Center has launched many satellites into orbit. Anything that circles the earth without falling out of space is called a satellite. A satellite is in orbit when it is circling the earth.

Some satellites ride into orbit in space shuttles. And some space shuttles have

The *Mariner 2* satellite (above) sent
back pictures of Venus in 1962.
Mariner 10 (right) photographed
Venus and Mercury in 1973.

brought satellites back
from orbit to the space
center.

Kennedy Space Center
has launched many
spaceships to the moon
and to other planets. Years

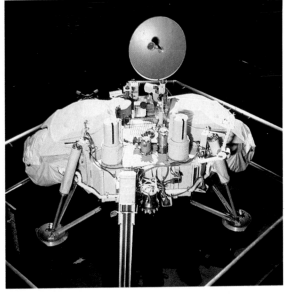

Lunar modules (left) landed astronauts on the moon. A *Viking* satellite traveled to Mars in 1976.

ago, astronuats landed on the moon and explored parts of it. Spaceships controlled from Earth have landed on Mars. Others have flown past the planets Mercury, Venus, Jupiter, Saturn, and Uranus.

WILDLIFE AND HISTORY

Merritt Island is home to more than just spaceships. Much of it is a wildlife refuge. Many rare animals live on the island's beaches, or in its saltwater marshes and ponds.

Pelicans, bald eagles, and manatees (sea cows) are a few of the rare animals that live there. Alligators live there, too.

Flocks of birds nest on Merritt Island.

Tribes of Native Americans were the first people on Merritt Island and Cape Canaveral. They hunted and fished there thousands of years ago. There are still mounds of earth where they buried their dead, and piles of

shells from the shellfish they ate.

Explorers from Spain gave Cape Canaveral its name more than four hundred years ago. They noticed fields of sugarcane growing there and gave it a Spanish name that means "cane field."

FIRST FLIGHT
FROM THE CAPE

Rockets are launched
from concrete launchpads.
The United States Air
Force began building the
first launchpad on Cape
Canaveral in 1949. It
launched its first rocket
there on July 24, 1950.

The Air Force tested new
rockets by launching them

Aerial view of launchpad at the Kennedy Space Center

over the ocean. That is the
safest way to test rockets.
Ships are warned to stay
away when rockets are
launched.

THE SPACE RACE

In the 1950s, America and Russia both were testing rockets. The tests turned into a race. Which nation would be the first to put a satellite in orbit? Which would be the first to send a person into space?

Russia launched the first satellite, *Sputnik 1,* on October 4, 1957.

The United States tried to launch its first satellite

A Jupiter rocket (left) carried *Explorer 1* into orbit.
Russia's *Sputnik 1* (above) was the first satellite in space.

on December 6, 1957. The rocket rose three feet. Then it fell back on its pad and exploded. The U.S. Army finally put a small satellite named *Explorer 1* into orbit on January 31, 1958.

BIRTH OF NASA

The National Aeronautics and Space Administration (NASA) came into being on October 1, 1958. NASA was put in charge of America's space programs. NASA set up its space center at Cape Canaveral.

In December 1958, NASA told of its plan to send a man into space. It called this plan Project Mercury. The *Mercury*

spaceship would be a little
capsule shaped like a bell.
Only one astronaut could
fit into it at a time.

A rocket would shoot the
capsule into space. Then
small rockets on the
capsule would slow it
down. It would land on the
ocean with the help of
parachutes.

But Russia was first
again. On April 12, 1961,
Yuri A. Gagarin became
the first man in space. He

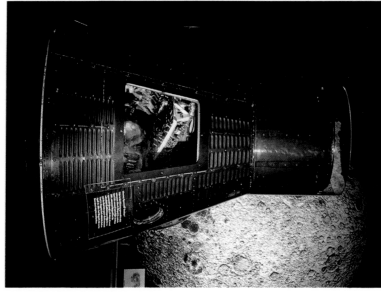

Astronaut Alan B. Shepard, Jr. (left)
flew into space in *Freedom 7* (above).

circled the earth once in a
space capsule, *Vostok 1.*

America launched its
first space traveler on
May 5, 1961. His name
was Alan B. Shepard, Jr.
He traveled 302 miles in

Cosmonaut Yuri Gagarin was the first human to orbit the earth.

15 minutes. It was a good flight. But it was not as exciting as Russia's. Americans felt they were losing the space race.

A NEW PLAN

On May 25, 1961,
President John F. Kennedy
told Americans about a
new space plan. He said:

> I believe that this nation
> should commit itself to
> achieving the goal, before this
> decade is out, of landing a
> man on the moon and
> returning him safely to earth.

America would need a
big, new rocket and a new
spaceship to send a man
to the moon. And it would

The Vehicle Assembly Building at Kennedy Space Center

need a new space center
to launch the rocket.

Cape Canaveral had no
room left for such big
rockets. NASA decided to
build a new space center
on Merritt Island.

PROJECT APOLLO

NASA called its moon plan Project Apollo. First there would be several *Apollo* test flights. Then an *Apollo* capsule would carry three astronauts into orbit around the moon and bring them back to earth.

From the capsule NASA would launch an *Apollo* spaceship called the lunar module. The lunar module would land on the moon with two of the astronauts from the capsule.

Both spaceships would ride into space on a *Saturn 5* rocket. The *Saturn 5* would stand as tall as a thirty-six-story building. It would be the most powerful rocket ever built.

The new space center would have to be huge to handle such big rockets. The moon rockets would

be put together in a building called the Vehicle Assembly Building. A crawler as big as a house would move the rocket to a launchpad. The launchpads would be more than three miles from the control center. This would keep people in the center safe from the blast of the rocket engines.

THE DOOR TO THE MOON

It took thousands of workers five years to build the new space center. President Kennedy never lived to see it. He was shot to death on November 22, 1963. The space center was named in his memory.

On the morning of May 21, 1969, the Vehicle Assembly Building opened one of its great doors.

Inside stood a *Saturn 5* rocket. High on top of the rocket sat the lunar capsule *Apollo 11.*

A crane lifts the *Apollo* spacecraft.

The crawler moved the rocket through the doorway on four pairs of tracks. The crawler moved very slowly to keep the rocket steady. It took seven hours to crawl three-and-a-half miles from the building to the launchpad.

The *Saturn 5* rocket lifts off (left). The *Apollo* command and service module (right) orbited the moon.

THE FIRST
MOON LANDING

Apollo 11 blasted off on July 16, 1969. Four days later, astronaut Michael Collins circled the moon in

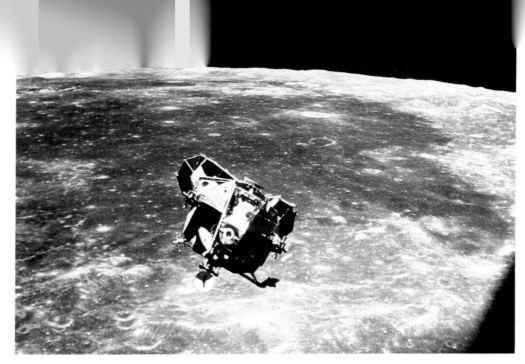

The earth rises over the moon's horizon.

the capsule while the other
two astronauts, Neil
Armstrong and Edwin
Aldrin, Jr., flew down to the
moon's surface in the lunar
module. Neil Armstrong
became the first man to
set foot on the moon. They

Close-up of
the lunar
module on
the moon

all got back safely. They
brought rocks from the
moon with them.

The space center
launched six more flights
to the moon over the next
three years.

SKYLAB AND SOYUZ

On May 14, 1973, a *Saturn 5* carried a different kind of spaceship. It was a space station named *Skylab. Skylab* was a place where three

Skylab (left) was launched in 1973. In 1975, a Soviet *Soyuz* spaceship (right) met with an American *Apollo* capsule.

astronauts could live for weeks at a time.

Americans and Russians met in space on July 15, 1975. The meeting was carefully planned. A Russian *Soyuz* spaceship and an American *Apollo* capsule joined together. Two Russians and three Americans visited each other for two days. Then they separated and landed in their own capsules.

Three different crews

Astronaut Thomas P. Stafford (top) greets Cosmonaut Aleksey A. Leonov.

lived in *Skylab*. Then it was abandoned. In 1979 it fell out of orbit. Part of it burned up like a meteor. The rest fell over Australia and the Indian Ocean. No one was hurt.

THE SHUTTLE DISASTER

On April 12, 1981,
Kennedy Space Center
launched a new kind of
spaceship—the space
shuttle *Columbia*. Unlike

the capsules, *Columbia* was made to be reusable. It had wings and three large rocket engines.

Columbia was the first of four space shuttles. After it came *Challenger*, *Discovery*, and *Atlantis*.

NASA was proud of its shuttle fleet. But in 1986 the worst tragedy in NASA's history claimed the *Challenger*.

On January 28, *Challenger* headed for space with a crew of

seven. One was Christa McAuliffe of Concord, New Hampshire. She was the first schoolteacher ever to fly in a space shuttle. Seventy-three seconds into its flight, *Challenger*'s fuel tank suddenly exploded in a huge fireball. None of the seven survived.

Kennedy Space Center will continue to launch space shuttles. In coming years, space shuttles will carry parts of a new space station into orbit.

But the people who work at the space center will never forget the *Challenger* or the seven who took its last flight. Every year on January 28, they will pause for one minute to remember them:

From left, front, are: Michael J. Smith, Francis R. (Dick) Scobee, and Ronald E. McNair; left, rear: Ellison S. Onizuka, Sharon Christa McAuliffe, Gregory Jarvis, and Judith A. Resnik.

Gregory Jarvis
Christa McAuliffe
Ronald E. McNair
Ellison S. Onizuka
Judith A. Resnik
Francis R. (Dick) Scobee
Michael J. Smith

45

WORDS YOU SHOULD KNOW

astronauts(AST • roh • nawts) — American space travelers
booster rocket(BOO • ster ROCK • et) — an initial rocket stage that boosts (that is, lifts or pushes) a spacecraft into flight
capsule(KAP • sul) — a small enclosed spaceship
crawler(KRAWL • er) — a huge vehicle that moves slowly on chain tracks to carry rockets and spaceships from an assembly building to a launchpad
launchpad(LAWNCH • pad) — a concrete platform or surface from which rockets or other spaceships are launched
lunar(LOON • er) — pertaining to the moon
meteor(MEET • ee • er) — a small piece of space matter that becomes visible when it burns up as it falls into the earth's atmosphere
module(MAWJ • yool) — a separate unit that is part of a spaceship
orbit(OR • bit) — the path an object takes as it moves around another object
satellite(SAT • ul • eyet) — a man-made object that orbits the earth without falling from space
shuttle(SHUT • til) — a vehicle that carries cargo or people over a prearranged route
Skylab(SKY • lab) — an orbiting space laboratory, large enough to carry several crew members
space station(SPAISS STAY • shun) — an artificial satellite on which people can live and work

INDEX

About the author

Timothy R. Gaffney is the military affairs and aviation writer for the Dayton Daily News *and* The Journal Herald, *publications of Dayton Newspapers, Inc. In 1986, Dayton Newspapers sent him to Kennedy Space Center to report on the Challenger space shuttle accident. He lives in Miamisburg, Ohio, with his wife Jean and three children, Kimberly, Christine, and Mark.*

7446

INDEX

About the author

Timothy R. Gaffney is the military affairs and aviation writer for the Dayton Daily News *and* The Journal Herald, *publications of Dayton Newspapers, Inc. In 1986, Dayton Newspapers sent him to Kennedy Space Center to report on the* Challenger *space shuttle accident. He lives in Miamisburg, Ohio, with his wife Jean and three children, Kimberly, Christine, and Mark.*

7446